Considering Children's Art:

why and how to value their works

Brenda S. Engel

National Association for the Education of Young Children, Washington, D.C.

Art credits: Gay Repast by Paul Klee (1928/29), page 13. Private collection. Reproduced by permission. Children's drawings and paintings courtesy of the author.
Cover art: painting by Adam, age 6.

National Association for the Education of Young Children
1509 16th Street, NW
Washington, DC 20036-1426
202-232-8777 or 800-424-2460
www.naeyc.org

Through its publications program the National Association for the Education of Young Children (NAEYC) provides a forum for discussion of major issues and ideas in the early childhood field, with the hope of provoking thought and promoting professional growth. The views expressed or implied are not necessarily those of the Association. NAEYC thanks the author, who donated much time and effort to develop this book as a contribution to the profession.

Library of Congress Catalog Card Number: 95-074821

ISBN 0-935989-70-6

NAEYC Order #102

Editor: Carol Copple; *Design and production:* Jack Zibulsky, Penny Atkins, and Danielle Hudson; *Copyediting:* Millie Riley; *Editorial Assistance:* Betty Nylund Barr and Anika Trahan

Printed in the United States of America

Contents

About the Author

Brenda S. Engel studied fine arts at Radcliffe College (now integrated into Harvard University). She began her professional life as an elementary school art teacher, first in a Friends school, later in a public school on an Army Air Force base. The opportunity, the first time quite serendipitous, to teach studio art four successive years at a week-long residential course for teachers in Leicestershire, England, led to new work as a consultant and advocate for "open education" in the United States. Based for the last 18 years at Lesley College in Cambridge, Massachusetts, Brenda Engel has taught and practiced qualitative evaluation, mostly of programs offered to school children by museums and other cultural institutions. Retired from active teaching, she is now a senior research associate at Lesley College, working with public schools on portfolio assessment. She is also a watercolorist.

Preface

The art of young children delights the observer because of its immediacy, freshness, unselfconscious directness. To most adults, relatively constrained by the expectations of those around them, the boldness and daring of child art seem enviably uncomplicated by anxiety about outcome or audience. The child appears fully identified with the work, almost continuous with it; the finished work shows the feelings, thoughts, and actions of the child in the doing. Because it is relatively unmediated by ulterior considerations, the work is a record, in the sense that a footprint is a record, conveying the presence of its maker.

For the child, making art is the actual process of formulating, organizing, and understanding experience—of making something of it. Art can give form and meaning to the puzzling, scary, interesting, funny, familiar, and unfamiliar things the child encounters in school, at home, on the street, on television, in books, in play. Given materials and opportunity, children will represent whatever is on their minds. For children the process is educational in the deepest sense. It allows them to explore—sort out—events and feelings they experience in daily life. For the adult viewer the product reflects the child—his or her knowledge, interests, concerns, and ways of going about dealing with a complex world. Children's creative work is one of the most valuable and deeply interesting sources of insight into children's minds.

Nonetheless, the creative arts are not generally valued in public education. During periods of tight budgets, elementary schools tend to cut back or eliminate programs in music, dance, and the visual arts. Some systems turn to parents to provide creative experiences for their children outside school, others apply for grants or rely on voluntary help. In many cases, although given up reluctantly, with genuine regret and often with public apology, the arts end up disappearing from both the school curriculum and the school department's budget.

Why does this happen? Why are the arts so often seen as nonessential, as frills or enrichment in the educational scheme? This book explores the reasons for the lack of weight accorded to a field with a 100-year history in America of significant theory and practice. Then it traces four general influences in this century on how we view the visual art of young children: that is, how we have come to understand the meaning of process and product to their lives and learning. Following from this discussion, the book offers suggestions on ways we can look at primary school-age children's creative visual work. My purpose is to reaffirm, along with many other advocates of child art, past and present, the importance of visual art in early schooling, then to provide some guides to its understanding and appreciation for adults who work and live with children.

* * *

I want to acknowledge the positive, informed response given the manuscript by Polly Greenberg; the prompt, intelligent queries by Carol Copple; and the expert copyediting by Millie Riley—all from the NAEYC editorial department.

—Brenda S. Engel

For our eight grandchildren—

artists all

1

Neglect of the Arts

At a recent educational conference some remarkably innovative and committed primary school teachers presented schemes they had developed in their schools or districts for assessing student learning. They had omitted art from the assessment plans altogether. It was as though the teacher-designers had simply forgotten about art as an activity to be taken seriously. Being both progressive and thoughtful, they were somewhat abashed when this considerable omission was pointed out but were still uncertain how to make amends. Actually, children in their classrooms did *do* both visual art and music, but when it came to assessment, these activities were left out, in effect giving them lower status. Thus, the arts are made vulnerable, even in the short run, to being cut at times of financial shortfall or when too many other demands are being made on the school or teacher's schedule. Omitting art from planning and assessment, in fact, is more the rule than the exception.

> The arts are simply not viewed as critical to the job of preparing young people for the work place—an attitude that was reflected in the six National Educational Goals announced by the president and the governors in 1990. No mention was made of the arts. (Horn & Sieder 1992, 53)

> Art is not generally seen as vital to a child's education, and it is commonly held that people need little or no formal education to experience, comprehend, and create art. (The Getty Center for Education in the Arts 1985, Introduction)

The tendency of the powers that govern educational practice—school boards, administrators, assessment programs—to neglect art education is puzzling, particularly since, even from a practical point of view, "visual thinking" (Arnheim 1969) is recognized as central to cognitive growth. Doing art is one of the important ways children learn about and make sense of the physical and social world around them.

David: I'd heard people talk about this thing. I think it was a praying mantis, but I didn't know what it was. So I looked at a book, and then I drew it, and then I knew what it was.

Juan: Or if you don't know what a wing is and how it's made you can draw it and then you know. (Gallas 1992, 23)

For each child it is important that his or her art be understood, commented on, appreciated—and taken as serious work.

Active engagement in art offers children a medium for self-expression, a way to validate their interests, perspectives, styles—in short, their ways of engaging with the world. Moreover, children—like adults—take in information or learn, that is, from what they see in the environment—not just what they hear, read, or see in two-dimension. Heightened awareness of the real world adds to their understanding and ability to discriminate.

Competence in art, too, can lead to broad opportunities after schooling—jobs and careers that depend on forms of visual thinking (advertising, television, film, illustration, layout, architecture, to name just a few). Images of all kinds surround us—both created and natural.

Rudolf Arnheim's statement on why the arts have low status in the curriculum still holds generally true in the mid-1990s: "They are based on perception, and perception is disdained because it is not assumed to involve thought" (1969, 3). The visual is not considered academic by school people in the way that reading and math are. The art of creative writing has relatively recently become validated in the curriculum through its recognized role in literacy learning. For most educators visual art seems not quite so necessary, rather an exercise of feeling than of thought.

An additional reason why art is not always valued in schools is because it is difficult to assess. Relatively few know how to do it—that is, how to look at the visual work of young children and have something direct and useful to say about it—not school administrators or parents, often not even teachers, and certainly not designers of assessment instruments. Comments such as, "Good job!" or "What a nice picture! Where should we put it up?" are benign but not always helpful or even satisfying. Adults can feel at a loss when confronted with a child's picture that appears familiar, seen many times before (e.g., a squarish house with triangular roof, lollipop flowers lined up on either side, and above a circle with radiating lines representing the sun). What is there to say? Actually, there is a lot to say, as we shall see in subsequent chapters.

For each child it is important that his or her art be understood, commented on, appreciated—and taken as serious work. Why? because art, like other human "works," is an outgrowth of self; it is imprinted with the character of the creator. The work of art, even a child's, constitutes "shared territory" (Himley 1991) between the artist and viewers, between the individual and the culture. As such, it merits and rewards respect and study. Close observation of art reveals something of the person—of what he or she sees as important, how he or she views and is attached to the surrounding world.

2

Changes in the Education Paradigm

Art contributes to learning in many subject areas; it is central to the kinds of abilities increasingly emphasized in contemporary thinking about education. Over the past three decades, there has been a paradigm shift in education. Educators have begun questioning the nature of all school subjects, redefining them as a result of new research and new social/political awareness. Reading is understood as the process of constructing meaning from print, not merely decoding print into oral or silent language. Writing is the creation of meaning through authentic communication, not primarily the practice of skills, such as spelling, handwriting, and punctuation.[1] Mathematics is built on basic understanding of structures and relationships for the purpose of solving problems. Social studies requires the exercise of multiple perspectives and imaginative engagement with the stories of peoples and events separated from oneself by time, space, and experience.

We are no longer content with the long-predominant transmission model of education that emphasizes a defined body of information and skills that teachers are responsible for transmitting to children. The selection of information itself (the curriculum) and the formation of beliefs about how skills should be taught no longer happen without question. What was once assumed as the common core of American education—Columbus as God-fearing, noble discoverer; the Pilgrims as bearers of religion and civilization to the natives; the cowboy as hero; the USA itself as

Children in many contemporary classrooms are actively involved in constructing meaning, thinking things out for themselves, and reinventing the world in their own terms. Making art draws on these ways of learning.

a melting pot—is, at the very least, being questioned. The content and direction of schooling has become an increasingly political subject. Although still appealing for its clarity and simplicity, as well as for its nostalgic associations (such as the one-room schoolhouse), the old transmission model of education does not fit the contemporary world; it no longer prepares children for the kinds of challenges they will encounter in their lives both in and out of school.

Even as the debate continues, however, children in many contemporary, forward-looking classrooms are actively involved in constructing meaning, thinking things out for themselves, and reinventing the world in their own terms. Making art draws on all of these ways of learning, most immediately through the acts of organizing, reflecting, judging, discriminating, selecting, and representing the raw material of the world. These thought functions are crucial to constructing meaning in every area of learning.

Classroom teaching—methods and content—is slow to change for multiple, complex reasons. Aware of the heavy responsibility they bear for their students' academic learning, as well as for their psychic and physical well-being, teachers do not undertake change lightly. In addition, they are constrained by the school culture, the hierarchical administrative structure within which they work, and they know that no matter what their beliefs they will be held accountable for students' test results.

The worth of new ideas and practices needs to be time tested. Many teachers, trained in traditional educational methods and having formed habits and procedures over the years around these methods, resist undertaking new ways. In the course of their careers, they have developed beliefs about learning, beliefs that guide their practice and that are hard to alter or relinquish without a sense of defeat, almost of self-betrayal. Many teachers also have become skeptical about the durability of new ideas, after years of experiencing fads and fashions that come and go.

In spite of these hindrances, change does take place. Classroom teaching has been perceptibly affected by—and has also contributed to—new conceptions of subject matter. Publishers of textbooks and related materials, too, have begun to align their products with the new definitions (although often only superficially).

In spite of the continuing dominance of standardized testing, the field of educational assessment has also begun to change along with new ideas about learning. Tests are seen as one contributing factor, no longer the whole story, and there has been a general reaction against their perceived overuse.

Current standardized tests are widely criticized for placing test-takers in a passive, reactive role rather than one that engages their capacities to structure tasks, produce ideas, and solve problems. Based on outmoded views of learning, intelligence, and performance, they fail to

> measure students' higher order cognitive abilities or to support their capacities to perform real-world tasks. (Darling-Hammond 1994, 11)

The key elements in the new-style assessments are referred to as "performance sampling," "exhibitions," "presentations," and "portfolios." These provide the data for what is termed *authentic assessment,* based on real-world tasks rather than on artificially constructed test items. Educators across the United States as well as in Canada, New Zealand, Australia, and the United Kingdom are developing systematic ways of collecting and learning directly from children's work, and children themselves are being encouraged to participate in reviewing and evaluating their products and in reflecting on their own progress in learning. Even very young children can be asked to talk about their work as long as the tone of the inquiry is positive, open, and accepting (see example on page 27). Children in the primary grades can select favorite pieces of work and be asked to explain the reasons behind their choices—the beginnings of self-evaluation.

Children's portfolios commonly contain a broad representation of work from all subject areas, including art. Teachers, however, have had more experience with, and are often more comfortable, helping students assess their progress in math and writing rather than visual art. An artwork presents a challenge: in what terms can it be assessed? How and what can we learn from the art of young children? It is a relatively easy matter to collect work and keep it systematically in a portfolio—once the issue of not sending everything home has been solved. But what then?

The answers lie, perhaps, in our reconsideration of art education and assessment together. Both the changes in conception of subject matter—particularly the emphasis on creativity and construction of meaning—and the changes in views of what constitutes worthwhile assessment invite such a reconsideration. The two interdependent discussions that follow—on ideas in this century that have influenced how child art is regarded and taught and the implications of these ideas for assessment—break into the self-enclosed dynamic: that an artwork is often not assessed in schools because teachers, like most people, usually don't know how to translate its value into words, in short, how to assess it.

For good reasons there is an aura of uneasiness around all the arts in regard to assessing their meanings. Works of art essentially make their own statements, and those statements are reduced when summarized in other terms. The quality and effect on the viewer of a Cezanne landscape, for example, cannot be adequately conveyed in words, nor can the emotions felt during a performance of Beethoven's Ninth Symphony.

Another reason to hesitate in judging works of art is that we have been so notoriously wrong on so many occasions—wrong about Picasso, wrong about Stravinsky, wrong about James Joyce, among many others. We don't want to be wrong once again, particularly about the work of children, the most vulnerable of artists.

Still, we can use language to describe works of art, to tell what is *there*—the lines, shapes, and colors in a painting; the notes, instruments, and time of a piece of music. This, in turn, can help the viewer to become more aware of the elements, qualities, and relationships and to see or hear and possibly understand the work more deeply in its own terms.

3

Historical Perspectives on Child Art

Not until the early 20th century did people begin to value children's art and other creative work, that is, to see these works as worthy of respect and serious study. Until then, children's work was measured in terms of how closely it approximated adult work. Child art had little apparent intrinsic interest of its own and in school was mostly a matter of handwriting and manual training through copying models.[2] Children were taught drawing and, sometimes, how to mix colors. The ability to draw, particularly, was recognized as advantageous, associated with high culture, useful (for girls) for practicing the decorative arts, and, above all, valuable discipline and training for its own sake. All of the qualities we have come to value in child art—originality, feeling, directness, economy of expression, symbolism, vividness, and so on did not enter the picture (so to speak).

What, then, brought about the dramatic change in how child art was regarded? Why did psychologists and educators begin to *see* and appreciate the spontaneous visual work of children? Why did parents begin to find their children's paintings worthy of space on the kitchen wall or their drawings suitable as Christmas greetings mailed out to friends and relatives? The scene was set for change at the turn of the century by the Child Study movement led by G. Stanley Hall. Hall's widely influential lectures and writings echoed across a century and a half, and from another country, the child-centered pedagogy of J.J. Rousseau. Writing before the French Revolution, in *Emile* Rousseau had urged parents and educators to pay attention to the nature

> *John Dewey recognized the close interconnections of thinking and feeling, both central to the production of art.*

of the child rather than to the corrupting demands of society and its institutions. Hall, too, saw the proper function of the school as supporting and responding to children's interests and natural ways of learning rather than expecting children to adjust to the schools' rigid, often arbitrary, subject matter and schedules. According to Hall and associates, close observation of children—child study—was the key to responsive educational planning, and children's artwork was included as a significant factor.[3] In the context of this new interest in and respect for childhood, the following discussion focuses on four large, 20th-century influences that generally affected how children's art—both process and product—has been viewed: John Dewey and progressive education; Freud and psychoanalysis; the Avant-Garde in art, for example, Paul Klee, Marc Chagall, Joan Miro, and Pablo Picasso; and, finally, developmental and cognitive psychology, represented here by Herbert Read, Viktor Lowenfeld, Rudolf Arnheim, Howard Gardner, and Patricia Carini. Of course, it was studio and classroom teachers who most directly shaped art education, but their attitudes and practices, as well as those of parents, were shaped, in turn, by influential thinkers and artists. These influences have, of course, intersected, interacted, and sometimes conflicted over the years. Their trickle-down effect on public education has been only partial: Some primary school classrooms have remained essentially 19th century in terms of art education—art still being a matter of coloring in worksheets, putting together precut shapes, and copying patterns. Nonetheless, the influence of these thinkers in this century has been pervasive. As a result of their speaking, writing, and doing, we have a deeper sense of the meaning of child art.

The overview that follows is highly selective, describing major forces or fields of influence on child art, without attempting to offer a comprehensive history of all the individuals who played a part in shaping or voicing each.

John Dewey and the progressive schools

John Dewey, the American empirical philosopher and educator, was concerned with democratizing the arts—bringing them into the arena of everyday life and experience.

> [The] task is to restore continuity between the refined and intensified forms of experience that are works of art and the everyday events, doings, and sufferings that are universally recognized to constitute experience. Mountain peaks do not float unsupported; they do not even just rest upon the earth. They are the earth . . . . (1934, 3)

Dewey criticized the generally held view of art as special and rarefied, isolated in museums, and produced only by professionals with privileged status. Consistent with his image of a truly democratic society, he advocated bringing the arts into everyday life. In school both fine arts and crafts were to be available to all children as fundamental means of expression and communication. In the progressive schools—the Laboratory School at the University of Chicago begun by Dewey himself and other schools influenced by his thinking—art was valued equally with other subject matter.

The principal of the Lincoln School, the progressive laboratory school for Teachers College in New York City, for example, described the curriculum as three interlocking circles: natural environment (sciences), social environment (social sciences), and human expression and communication (the arts) (Dix 1939). The three circles were given equal weight in the curriculum.[4] Children's art was taken seriously, regarded as authentic, worthwhile, and valuable on its own terms.

Art by children was conspicuous in the offices, meeting rooms, halls, and classrooms of the progressive school in the '20s and '30s. By all accounts art made its own case then: that is, the paintings, drawings, collages, murals, ceramics, and constructions by children on display were both interesting and beautiful. They showed that if the school supports and believes in the value of children's art, children can and will produce wonderful work.[5]

John Dewey recognized the close interconnections of thinking and feeling, both central to the production of art. Subject matter could be exciting, in part because it evoked past associations, bringing to a level of consciousness half-buried thoughts and feelings. Art provided a way of giving these form, making them available and communicable. Thus art activity had a therapeutic benefit along with intellectual and social value.

> To be set on fire by a thought or scene is to be inspired. What is kindled must either burn itself out, turning to ashes, or must press itself out in material that changes the latter from crude metal into a refined product. Many a person is unhappy, tortured within, because he has at command no art of expressive action. (Dewey 1934, 65)

In other words, lack of an appropriate outlet for expressing strong feelings, no matter what their origin, results in frustration and unhappiness.

The influence of Freud and psychoanalysis

Educators influenced by Freudian psychology might not have allowed Dewey's assumption that "what is kindled" can simply "burn itself out." Rather, they subscribed to the belief that strong feelings will out, finding expression eventually in some form. Psychoanalytically oriented educators became interested in mental health in schools and saw art as playing a crucial role in its maintenance—a way of providing access to, and allowing expression of, repressed feelings.

Margaret Naumburg, founder in 1914 and codirector of the Children's School (later renamed The Walden School) in New York

City, was one of the first to change classroom practice in response to the new psychology. Naumburg, who had been psychoanalyzed, was primarily interested in promoting children's mental health in school rather than in teaching traditional subject matter. The school was designed as a free, nonrepressive environment in which children would be able to express themselves and learn in healthy, natural ways. Teachers, called by their first names, were less authoritarian than those in traditional schools and seen more as guides and allies than as agents for control. In fact, the very word *control* was for many progressive educators an anathema, almost synonymous with *repression.*

The Walden School encouraged free exploration and expression in all areas of learning. In art, children chose their own media and subject matter. Not only was the idea of art lessons eliminated, but adults were reluctant to correct, judge, or react to children's work at all for fear of inhibiting spontaneous expression. Art as therapy came first and art as aesthetic experience second, although the two purposes were inseparable in practice.

> The faculty—at least half of whom had undergone analysis at the urging of Miss Naumburg—tended to emphasize the arts, arguing that artistic creations serve to bring into conscious life the buried material of the child's emotional problems. (Cremin 1961, 213)

Again, art was at the center of school life, although the emphasis was somewhat different from John Dewey's. Both Naumburg and Dewey saw art activities as fundamental to the mental health of the individual, but Dewey emphasized it more as an aspect of community experience and Naumburg, as an outlet for repressed feelings of the individual. Together, however, the views of the two educators influenced everyday practice in the progressive schools and, eventually, to some extent that in other private and public schools around the country.

There was, unsurprisingly, a strong backlash of suspicion, hostility, and skepticism toward the new beliefs. Critics attacked John Dewey and progressive education for fostering communism and free love, catering to the privileged classes, and also undermining traditional educational values and discipline. Freud and Freudianism, seen as hand-in-glove with progressive education, were also attacked and lampooned, their ideas found far-fetched and embarrassing; nonetheless, views on child art were permanently affected. In spite of ongoing traditional practices in many schools, the general consciousness changed, and children's art, wherever it was allowed to flourish, dramatically proved its own worth.

The Avant-Garde in art

A third influence that indirectly and unintentionally lent legitimacy to children's ways of seeing and representing the world came from artists themselves. Avant-Garde painters, from Paul Gauguin on, began to look for inspiration in the direct, untutored art of less-sophisticated cultures, including that of childhood. By the turn of the century, a number of European artists, influenced by the Impressionists and Post-Impressionists, were turning away from *realism*. Paul Klee (1879–1940) is a case in point. A highly conscious, intellectual, and original artist, Klee struggled as a young man to overcome the destructive effects of what he perceived as a "compromise with realism." By his own account, nature and naturalism were hazards for the artist.

> Nature had already become a useful crutch which I was then forced to use too long, I would say until the year 1911 inclusively. (1964, 147)
>
> My work doesn't progress too well, as if the study of nature had poisoned it somehow. (1964, 151)

Klee's art is not childish. Nonetheless, his brilliant, subtle, mature work does have some characteristics in common with child art, some unmistakable affinities. Klee, in his efforts to move beyond the constraints, as he saw them, of naturalism, used pictorial techniques that remind us of child art, of the work of young drawers and painters who have not yet gotten to the point of having to deal with these constraints; children are free of the laws of perspective because they don't know they exist. Klee, on the other hand, had to overcome considerable training in order to represent experience in the fresh, direct, and significant ways he aimed for.

By the 1920s Klee had freed himself to use simplified, deeply meaningful, and representative, rather than narrowly realistic, images arranged in flattened space. In much of Klee's work, figures do not overlap, and there is little suggestion of hierarchy or relative importance. An example, *Gay Repast* (1928/29) (see page 13), is a composition of 15 objects, each one discrete (although two telephone-receiverlike objects are connected by crossed lines): a bottle labeled "cognac"; a goblet slightly tipped to the left, with liquid (presumably cognac) pouring out; a shell in a bowl; a fork with five tines; an egg-shaped form; a flag decorated with crossed diagonal lines; three circular disks; the telephone receivers; a house decorated with the number five, two windows, and triangles on the roof; and a doll-like figure with a chess piece (castle) on its head. Near the center is a vertical idol-like, mouselike figure with whiskers, large ears, and diamond-shaped eyes. The reminders of child art in this painting include the separation of the objects, the unabashed and front-facing clarity of each one, the arrangement (including the fact that the objects are given almost equal value in the composition), the lack of apparent gravity, the general flatness of the depiction, and the multiple perspectives. Although highly conscious qualities—the result of Klee's more than 20 years of experience and artistic struggle—these contribute to an overall impression of directness and conscious, intentional naiveté. In this work as well as in many other Klee drawings and paintings, there is a sense of playfulness that we associate with childhood, although not necessarily with child art. Children's drawings often seem funny to adults: a man, for example, drawn as a wavery circle enclosing four irregular shapes (features), forklike arms sticking out from where one would expect ears. But the intention is serious—to work out and communicate a concept.

It might be said that the direction of Klee's artistic development was opposite to that of most children: his work moves, over the years, away from the appearance of things, while child art develops toward it. Klee himself seemed to recognize an intersection between the two lines of development in a single, somewhat mysterious, unprepared for but resonant entry in his diary:

> A good moment in Oberhofen. No intellect, no ethics. An observer above the world or a child in the world's totality. The first unsplit instant in my life. (1964, 190)

Others of the 20th-century Avant-Garde, in addition to Paul Klee (e.g., Kandinsky, Miro, Chagall, Picasso), inadvertently helped create an atmosphere of acceptance and positive pleasure in the directness and spontaneity characteristic of the art of young children. It is a short step indeed from the work of Matisse and other Avant-Garde artists to drawings like Aurora's couch (see page 14). If Picasso could present simultaneous views in the same portrait (both eyes on the same side of the head), a child's drawing of a house with all four sides visible might be seen as interesting and inventive rather than just plain wrong. Observers were freed to appreciate child art for its authenticity, economy of means, and expressiveness. Picasso himself reportedly said, "Once I drew like Raphael, but it has taken me a whole lifetime to learn to draw like children" (Gardner 1980, 8).

Art and development

Recognition of the relationship of art to children's thought and development is crucial to the status of art education in the elementary school curriculum. The case for art may come to rest on the perception that art can contribute to children's learning and thinking and, more narrowly, to their academic success. The role of art in cognitive development has been extensively explored in the 20th century by a number of philosophers and psychologists. Many articulated a set of categories, hierarchies, or taxonomies for classifying children's art. A few of the most important of these are noted here (the author's own scheme appears in Chapter 6).

Although there had been attempts to outline developmental stages in child art since the late-19th century, the British psychologist Cyril Burt (1940) was one of the first to specify in detail a series of developmental stages, with his aim to establish norms of human intelligence for testing purposes.[6] Some of Burt's seven developmental stages[7] are similar to contemporary formulations:

Gay Repast *by Paul Klee.*

A couch by Aurora, age 6.

- scribble (ages 2–5).
- line (age 4): Children develop more control and intention.
- descriptive symbolism (ages 5–6): Children begin to use schema for the human figure, which is drawn with some logic.
- descriptive realism (ages 7–8): Children's art is still based on what they know rather than what they see.
- visual realism (ages 9–11): Children begin to draw from nature.
- repression (ages 11–14): Children frequently become discouraged and frustrated at their inability to draw realistically.
- artistic revival (early adolescence): Children's drawing begins to resemble adult work.

Herbert Read, writing in the 1940s, was skeptical about Burt's stages: "My own observations do not altogether support such a neat evolutionary theory" (Read [1943] 1956, 123). Read criticized Burt for his neglect of the "correlation of expression and temperament" and for Burt's notion of the child as a "universal norm." Read was primarily interested in the relationship of character to art. After examining several thousand children's drawings, Read identified many stylistic characteristics that he eventually consolidated and grouped under eight headings: organic, empathetic, rhythmical pattern, structural form, enumerative, haptic, decorative, and imaginative. These characteristics he then matched to Jung's ([1938] 1971) psychological types.[8] For instance, Read associated Jung's feeling/extrovert type with decorative art, Jung's feeling/introvert type with more imaginative kinds of work (Read [1943] 1956, 147).

Although Read denied that his classifications were clear-cut or exclusive and affirmed that the basic key to understanding the child was still "insight and intuition," he saw "temperament" as a consistent, identifiable factor. He believed "it might be possible to construct a graphic key to temperament, so that the individual psychological constitution could be identified with reasonable accuracy by the teacher (somewhat on the lines of a scientific graphology such as becomes possible in later life)" ([1943] 1956, 158).

Although one might have doubts about typing artworks in this way (as well as about the validity of "scientific graphology"), Read's categories add a broadening dimension, beyond the purely developmental, to our ways of looking at children's art. Also, Read did take child art very seriously. His comprehensive and influential book *Education Through Art* makes a case for art as the basic approach to teaching and learning. Read was one of the first to validate child art in its own terms, unlike Cyril Burt, who saw children's work as a series of awkward steps toward competent and realistic adult art. Read described "the child's graphic activity" as a "specialized medium of communication with its own characteristics and laws . . . not determined by canons of objective visual realism, but by the pressure of inner subjective feeling or sensation" ([1943] 1956, 135). The essential response of young artists was neither to how things are perceived nor to what is known about them, but to how things feel.

In the same decade, Viktor Lowenfeld published a widely influential work, which still has considerable presence in the field of art education (Lowenfeld [1947] & Brittain 1967). Echoing Read's validation of children's work as interesting and worthwhile in its own right, Lowenfeld also emphasized its importance to elementary education. In most school subjects, children were asked to come up with right answers, everyone to arrive at the same solution (no longer, of course, considered a reasonable assumption, even in history or mathematics). Art, in Lowenfeld's view, was virtually unique in emphasizing original solutions or "divergent thinking." By the same logic, Lowenfeld inveighed against coloring books, against the imposition of adult standards, against "forced" competition, and against grading of children's art—all of these harmful to the "tender beginnings" of creativity.

In describing developmental stages in art, Lowenfeld emphasized their function in education in ways that seem quite contemporary: "[The] study of a child's creative works is made by the teacher to gain insight into the child's growth and not in order to confront him with his weaknesses or strengths" ([1947] 1967, 53). Growth was broadly conceived to include emotional, intellectual, physical, perceptual, social, and aesthetic factors. The stages described by Lowenfeld had some similarities to those that came before:

- scribbling (ages 2–4)
- pre-schematic (ages 4–7)
- schematic (ages 7–9)
- dawning realism (ages 9–11)
- pseudo-naturalistic (ages 11–13)
- crises of adolescence (ages 13–17)

Each stage described was detailed in terms of conceptual understanding, expressiveness, aesthetic quality, psychology, and motivational factors.

4

Contemporary Views

Contemporary psychologists, recognizing the therapeutic and cognitive aspects of child art, as well as its genuine aesthetic value, have built on and extended the insights of writers such as Dewey, Naumburg, Read, and Lowenfeld. With its importance established, children's art posed a number of intriguing questions: Where do the ideas come from that children are interested in respresenting at various ages? What is the relationship between seeing and thinking? Do children see the world as adults see it? Is the urge to represent innate? Which aspects of art are common to all children and which are particular to the individual child? What role does art play in education?

Art as visual thinking

It remained for Rudolf Arnheim (1969) to justify in theoretical terms the cognitive value of art, asserting that vision is actually a form of thinking rather than merely a sensory modality that aids thinking. Arnheim believes it important to understand "visual perception" as "visual thinking" in order to counteract the common, historically derived assumption that activities such as mathematics and language involve thinking but that art, belonging to the realm of the senses, is relatively mindless. The common notion of the eye as a recording device that delivers raw data to the brain, which then makes sense of them, gives perception a bad name, reducing it to a mechanical activity separate from thought.

Arnheim defines perception as a cognitive or organizing activity that makes sense of the literal, cameralike images reflected on the retina. Perception involves cognitive operations, he says, like "active exploration, selection, grasping of essentials, simplification, abstraction, analysis and synthesis, completion, correction, comparison, problems-solving, as well as combining, separating, putting in context"—all of these "mental operations involved in the receiving, storing, and processing of information" (1969, 13). An example of visual thinking is correcting a retinal image: a person on the other side of the room is perceived as roughly the same size as a person nearby, even though the nearby figure may take up a good deal more space on the retina.

"The young mind generates the impulse to take hold of the world, to understand it, and to bear witness to its wondrous wealth." (Arnheim 1989, 18)

In doing art, children represent—feel, think, visualize—their experience. As with language, children's forward motion toward organization and making sense of the world, of perceiving more, is evident. For early language users, a single word can stand for a whole set of things (*doggie* for anything with four legs that moves). For young children, also, a shape drawn on paper can represent a number of things with a similar structure. A generic animal, for example, often first appears as a roughly circular shape (head), attached at the side to a larger circular shape (body), with a series of four or more vertical lines going down from the larger shape (legs). Later on, an elongated diagonal loop representing a neck might appear between the head and body to make the animal into a giraffe, or an upward-curved loop attached to the front of the head is added to make the creature an elephant. Children gradually make (perceive) finer distinctions.

Arnheim's later thinking remains consistent with his earlier work.

> Once we understand vision as an inseparable aspect of the organism's way of coping with the relevant features of reality, we know that all such cognition starts with the most general aspect of things and proceeds from there gradually to images as particular as the purpose requires. For many needs of the young mind, a few broad features of things are all that is called for, and correspondingly a pictorial rendering of such elementary traits is all that needs to be given. Father and mother are sufficiently distinguished in a pair of trousers and a skirt. (Arnheim 1989, 17)

For Arnheim, early scribbles are "manifestations of mind," ways of understanding experience.

> The young mind generates the impulse to take hold of the world, to understand it, and to bear witness to its wondrous wealth. Once we have acquired the respect for this early achievement, we shall never underestimate the importance of art work at any level of human maturity, be it in the school child or in the adult artist. (1989, 18)

Pablo Picasso, like Arnheim, saw art as a means of formulating experience:

> Let it be understood above all that the artist works by necessity . . . like all of us, he lives by working on his environment. His inveterate curiosity makes him try to see purposes and meaning in his world. He uses art as a mode of thinking about and giving form to his experience. (Field 1970, 20)

The process of creating works of art is, thus, a process of giving form to experience. Experience, however, has to be understood more broadly than as concept development and cognition only; it also involves feelings, skill with the medium, values (what seem important to the individual), characteristic gesture and style, personal aesthetic. All these add to the object created. Arnheim describes how training in the arts contributes to other studies, claiming that "there is hardly any teaching and learning in any field of study without the practical use of imagery" (1989, 30). The kind of thinking exercised in creating art—particularly the need to relate the particular to the abstract—applies to all disciplines:

> By coping with [structural problems] on the more tangible terrain of perceptual organization one can become more skillful in tackling organizational problems elsewhere in life. (Arnheim 1989, 18)

The work of Sylvia Fein both supports and broadly illustrates Arnheim's view of art thinking. She has collected examples of "first drawings" (including those of children) from many places and many times (Fein 1993)—carved on rock faces and tombstones, etched on vases, painted on the walls of caves, woven into cloth patterns, or drawn with pencil on paper. As humans we all start off with a strikingly similar visual vocabulary, which Fein characterizes as the "fundamentals of artistic structure:

- meanders
- circles
- concentric circles
- spirals
- arcs
- radiating, parallel, perpendicular, and oblique lines" (1993, 134)

These forms, the building blocks of art, develop first as ideas, not as responses to the environment. A drawn circle is a concept, the expression of something envisioned rather than a response to something seen. In her earlier writing, Fein describes Heidi, age 4, discovering the circle.

> The coiling motion leads to Heidi's next innovation. Starting at a point on the paper, she encloses an area with a single line and returns to the starting point, producing the simplest, most balanced of all forms, the circle. Once Heidi has created the circle, she never again scribbles . . . . Having discovered circles, Heidi draws them in various sizes and in every relationship she can devise. On every available piece of paper, and on some less appropriate surfaces, appear small circles within circles, circles on the edges of circles, and circles within circles within circles. (1974, 18–19)

Like Heidi, children will repeat, practice, vary, and elaborate circles and, inevitably, at some point use them to represent an element of the visible world. A round shape with radial lines (the common mandala) can represent the sun, a face, a human figure, or simply a satisfying decoration. In the common order of events, the form is discovered before its applications.

The developmental research psychologist Howard Gardner also assumes, and builds on Arnheim's claim, that art is an "activity of the mind" (1990, 9). Beginning in the 1960s Gardner has worked to synthesize two kinds of theory: Piaget's developmental stage

The "eruption of artistry" among 5- to 7-year-olds—in music and dance, block building, and storytelling, as well as in drawing and painting—seems to stem from their new command of the expressive media.

theory of learning and the work of philosophers of symbolic forms—particularly Ernst Cassirer (1957), Suzanne Langer (1942), and Nelson Goodman (1968).

Infants and young children learn about the world in natural, intuitive ways through interaction with their social and physical environment. Along with Arnheim, Gardner believes that in their early representative drawings, children create an equivalent in graphic form of their conception of an object. "A general correspondence suffices between what is drawn and the object in the world" (Gardner 1980, 63). Drawing, a natural symbol-making activity, is, according to Gardner, a path to knowing, a means of learning. He traces the development of children's art from the early, apparently random marks made by the very young child through the beginnings of representation, "the eruption of artistry at the threshold of school" (1980, 94), to the often (according to Gardner) less-imaginative, less-interesting, but more-skilled work of children in the middle elementary years. "For it is pursuit of the realistic and the literally true which casts its spell on the individual in middle childhood" (1980, 142). Gardner attributes the "eruption of artistry" among 5- to 7-year-olds—in music and dance, block building, and storytelling, as well as in drawing and painting—to a new command of expressive media: the child, after several years of rehearsal, can manipulate materials intentionally in the service of his or her ideas (1980, 94). At the same time, the child is not yet constrained by a perceived need to make things look realistic.

Like Naumburg (1950) and the other early Freud-influenced educators, Gardner sees art activities as central to the child's psychological health. "[F]or youngsters four to seven years of age, graphic media present a uniquely rich, flexible, and personal means for exploring the depths of interpersonal relations and personal feelings" (1980, 114). Art provides expressive means for children to work through issues of aggression, violence, and conflict and their own feelings of anxiety and helplessness in the world. Themes, once more commonly represented in myth, folktale, and fairy tale, are now also encountered in the artifacts of popular culture—such as Star Wars and Batman. Children in their artwork repeat and elaborate all of these heroes (and opposing villains) (Gardner 1980).

Carini and the Prospect School: Children's "works"

During the three decades in which Howard Gardner carried out much of his research—the '60s, '70s, and '80s—Patricia Carini and colleagues at the Prospect School in Vermont also were observing children's work closely, although from a different perspective.[9] Carini's primary interest was in the child as revealed through his or her actions and works over time. In this sense Carini represents something of a return to Herbert Read's interest in personality, although her understanding is subtler and deeper. She never sought to catalog types but to gain insight into the ways a particular child engaged with the world, including with formal learning. The keys to understanding, for Carini, were direct observation and reflection: observation, that is, of both the child and the child's works and individual or group reflection on those observations. Carini broadly defined the child's works to include writing, talk, play, construction, music, and the visual arts.

Margaret Himley, who has worked with and written with and about Carini, locates children's writings "within the permeable border region of child and culture" (Himley 1991, 7). To understand children as writers, she further proposes "dwelling in that space" and "reading—carefully, slowly, descriptively, dialogically—the many texts they have written over time and in various settings" (1991, 8). Children's visual works are seen as occupying the same space, the same "border region," and at the Prospect School were accorded the same kind of close and continuing attention as children's writing and other creative work.

For more than two decades, Carini and colleagues, individually and in groups, spent many hours dwelling in that border region, collecting and reflecting on children's work. They developed formats for reflective processes—ways members of a group could describe to themselves children's work and could reach a deep level of appreciation for and insight into it. Each person brings to this group process a wide range of personal references from both interior and exterior sources: his or her own memories of childhood, experience with children and schooling, knowledge of literature (from poetry and novels to philosophy and psychology), and art, as well as other kinds of experiences in the world. Taking off always from a description of the piece of work before the group—what can actually be seen—the discussion usually moves of its own accord in the direction of interpretation. However, by staying within the compass of the piece of work itself, comments are controlled by it. Ungrounded speculation is discouraged. Participants take turns commenting on what they see, adding their own perceptions, frequently triggered by those of others and, in turn, triggering theirs. Each person adds; no one contradicts or argues. At intervals a chairperson summarizes the discussion, accommodating and restating the full range of reactions without attempting a reconciliation or synthesis. The summation at the end leaves the work intact, still speaking for itself, not identified with a developmental level or reduced to an immature version of adult art. In the end participants' knowledge and appreciation of the work seem remarkably expanded and deepened.

Art at the Prospect School was a central activity—a path to learning in the broadest sense and a source of clues for the emergent curriculum (inseparable as both subject matter and context for the teaching of skills). The children's work, collected over the years, suggested their interests, deep and enduring themes, and characteristics of individual children. Along with recorded observations and reports, this work constituted the ongoing documentation of children's learning and personal development at the school.[10]

D.W. Winnicott, the British psychoanalyst, described a strikingly similar border region between child and culture that he defined as a "potential" space in which the related activities of play and art take place.

> The third part of the life of a human being, a part that we cannot ignore, is an intermediate area of experiencing, to which inner reality and external life both contribute. It is an area that is not challenged, because no claim is made on its behalf except that it shall exist as a resting-place for the individual engaged in the perpetual human task of keeping inner and outer reality separate yet interrelated. (1971, 2)

From Winnicott's view as child therapist, this space, this "intermediate area of experiencing," is crucial to the healthy development of the individual.

Some other ways of looking

There are many useful, valid ways of looking at and appreciating young children's art, many lenses through which viewers can assess its qualities. Over the past half century, a number of researchers and practitioners other than those already mentioned have thought and written about children's work, usually, although not exclusively, emphasizing a particular point of view. Only a few are briefly mentioned here to suggest the extent of the possibilities. Miriam Lindstrom (1957), among others, analyzed child art in terms of conceptual development and increasing skill and control over the medium, delineating common stages of "normal" development. Rhoda Kellogg (1969) actually cataloged from a large collection of examples the developmental characteristics of children's visual work. Jacqueline Goodnow (1977) investigated how children typically solve the problems of translating from the three-dimensional world around them to the two-dimensional world of pencil and paper.

All of these approaches have yielded useful insights. In addition, educators, inspired at times by Howard Gardner's (1983) theory of multiple intelligences (which includes spatial, akin to, visual intelligence), have explored the connections between art and other school-based disciplines. In a book on assessment for science, for example, George E. Hein and Sabra Price use children's drawings "to discover how an individual student thinks, what he has learned, what she feels" (1994, 87). Art educators Janet Olson (1992) and Karen Ernst (1994) are each concerned with the natural and mutually enhancing relationship between writing and art in school. Ernst describes her work as an attempt to "demonstrate the interactive continuity of visual and verbal modes of expression and the benefits their integration could have for visual children" (1994, 156). Karen Gallas, an elementary school teacher, integrates art activities into all aspects of the curriculum in her first-grade classroom, helping students gain insight into their own understanding. The resonant title of her seminal article is "Epistemology: Enabling Children to Know What They Know" (Gallas 1992).

The role art can play, in general, in adding meaning to other subject matter was recognized and written about during the era of "progressive education," as mentioned earlier. Later in the 1960s, the "open education" movement, influenced by the "integrated day" practices in British primary schools, also put the arts at the center of schooling, with connections to other subject areas. Children in open classrooms were encouraged to express their ideas and feelings in a variety of media, and teachers, taking the work seriously, learned to observe it with care and to gain from it deeper understanding of children's thinking. One of the early spokespersons for the integrated day practice, British school head Roy Illsley, however, related a cautionary tale in reporting a conversation with 6-year-old Jonathan, who had just finished a colorful painting of a sunset:

Illsley—That's a beautiful painting you've done there, Jonathan. If you're finished, perhaps you'd like to write about it now.

Jonathan (with some annoyance)—Mr. Illsley, if I had wanted to *write* about it, I would have *written* about it. I wanted to *paint* it! (1969)

American educators in the mid-1980s became aware of an example of schooling actually beginning with, and based on, art. The remarkable visual work produced by preschool children in the northern Italian district of Reggio Emilia was first introduced to American audiences through a traveling exhibit, "The Hundred Languages of Children." The accompanying catalog explains the pedagogy of the schools as "on the side of a genetic, constructivist and creative perspective" (1987, 18) and art as a language for which children have an inborn capacity. The children's art, which Reggio Emilia calls "the magnificent offerings of children," resulted from children's natural curiosity and perceptiveness. Doing art expanded these young children's understanding of the world, preparing them for more formal schooling later on. Observing children's artworks, both the process and product, allows teachers insight into how children are constructing the world.

Three little pigs, plus one, by Elektra, age 7.

5

Responses to Child Art

Knowledge often runs ahead of practice. In the field of education, particularly, more is known about good educational practice than is commonly demonstrated in the schools. This disparity is due, in equal part, to the natural conservatism of those responsible for the education and well-being of children, to the unfortunate gulf separating research and teaching, and to the politics and finances of educational administrations. Language arts and math continue to be the basic agenda for most programs in early education, although there are public and private schools that manage to sustain good art programs as well as many active advocacy groups that continue to support the arts in the schools. Preschool teachers do, however, generally recognize the value for children of creative work, and preschoolers create free, colorful, expressive visual work. Why and how does it disappear? How can parents and teachers talking with children about their work help to keep it going?

Art in public schools

In schools in the United States, children learn to put down their thoughts and experiences in writing. It takes a while, however, for them to develop this ability. Early on in preschool and kindergarten, children naturally begin symbolic representation—express meaning—on paper through drawing. In some schools young children actually keep daily journals in which they draw about what interests them. Letterlike shapes tend to appear gradually and spontaneously on the page, first as design elements scattered about, soon as strings of letters recognizable as such but often without easily decipherable meaning. At some point the letters, rather than continuing to function primarily as conventionalized

As they draw, children can simultaneously record and work out on paper their ideas and feelings about relationships, events, and the nature of things in general.

design elements, take on new function for the child: they are understood to represent the sounds of oral speech.

Later on when children begin more formal literacy learning (reading and writing), words are assigned a place on the page apart from the drawing. Primary grades' composition paper ordinarily has lines for writing on the bottom half of the paper, space for drawing on the top half. Words and images, however, continue to have equal and reciprocal meaning—the words, often in the form of captions or labels, serve to explain the drawing; the drawing expands the meaning of the words. In Elektra's artwork (see page 24), she uses pictures and words jointly to tell a story of three little pigs, plus one. Also, for example, Eduardo in grade one drew a picture of a basketball game. He drew a basket at the top of a pole on each side of the page, a ball about to drop into the basket on the left, and also the requisite number of players on each team, represented by stick figures. Across the top of the page he wrote, "Tne CELICS aND TnE BoLLS" (The Celtics and the Bulls). In this case the writing and drawing have equal importance: the title identifies the subject of the drawing, the drawing elaborates the meaning of the title.

Soon, in school settings drawings lose importance, becoming illustrations for the text—a secondary role. The text contains the *whole* story or explanation, with illustrations as add-ons, not strictly necessary. Before long, in fact, drawings and words, rather than being assigned different spaces on the page, are actually taught in different learning spaces in the school building—art in the art room, reading and writing in the classroom. Without common space the two activities lose common meaning. Art tends to be relegated to the realm of "feeling," reading and writing to "thinking." Art teachers, in schools fortunate enough to have them, continue teaching skills and encouraging art as expression; but reading and writing are understood as the real work of school, confirming Arnheim's analysis of art as, in general, being considered noncognitive.

A crayon drawing of a baseball game done by a 6-year-old, analyzed in the next chapter, gives an example of a child representing his experience of a complex phenomenon; it illustrates how children can simultaneously record and work out on paper their ideas and feelings about relationships, events, and the nature of things in general. The recording *is* the thinking out and feeling, just as for many writers formulation occurs not beforehand but in the act of writing. Formulation of experience, endowing it with personal and public meaning, is worked out on paper, in the doing itself. Perception is transformed, given heightened meaning (colored in) when turned into art.

Observing and talking with children

Parents and teachers, of course, have the advantage of being able to observe spontaneous art-in-the-making, an opportunity only sometimes open to researchers. Seeing a child actually engaged in "visual thinking" makes possible additional insights: the sequence in which the child puts lines or shapes on the paper, the amount of time spent, the degree of concentration and involvement, the creator's response to happy (or unhappy) accidents—like paint running down the paper. Some children characteristically become frustrated and abandon or throw away their work:

> Sam balled up and threw away one half-done painting after another, saying angrily, "I goofed!" His 4-year-old sister, a year younger than Sam, apparently undisturbed after accidentally dropping red paint in the middle of her picture, said, "That's all right—I'll make it into a flower."

Some children carry on a running commentary as they work:

> "Now I'm making a black road going all the way down here," Daren says, as he trails the brush down and off the paper onto the table.[11]

Children's comments can add to—or occasionally confuse—the viewer's understanding. Most parents, teachers, and researchers have the good sense to listen, observe, and not interrupt children with questions while they are working. It is a different story after they have finished. Then many children are often happy to talk about what they have done, although some may be reluctant and should not be urged.

What kinds of questions can adults ask? How does the interested adult open a conversation with a child about a piece of artwork? It is advisable not to leap to interpretation, certainly not to summary judgment. With all products of the creative imagination—adults' as well as children's—the easiest, least awkward, and usually the most useful approach is description: start with—and possibly end with—what is there, visible and describable. Such an approach is evident in the conversation between Will, age 3½, and his grandmother.

Grandmother: "I see you painted a big green shape here with three blue dots on it."

Will: "I think that is a three-eyed crab" (looking at and evidently deciding, ex-postfacto, what it was he had represented).

Grandmother: "What about the red lines?"

Will: "Well, that one up there that looks like an *S* is a Chinese dragon.

Grandmother: "A dragon like a Chinese kite?" (knowing Will had seen a picture of one recently in a book).

Will: "Yes. And the blue lines are all snakes. And down here (pointing to the lower left part of the paper)—all that messy stuff is where Clare messed it up."

Grandmother: "What about the purple squiggles between the snakes?"

Will: "Well, I painted those just because I wanted to."

Grandmother: "I see. It looks like you had fun painting that picture."

Will: "Well, I'm good at painting. And I want to eat something now" (end of conversation).[12]

Talking with children about their work can follow the same general sequence described later in this book for observing work without the children present: progress from what you see quite literally and how the work is organized to what it seems to be about. With the child present, however, he or she will (or possibly will not) offer an explanation or interpretation. In any event, description is not only a lead-in but sometimes is all that is necessary or advisable. Usually, in the art of young children, there is a lot to talk about, to describe, without either evaluating or interpreting meaning. But it does take time. Careful observation always takes time, which means that in busy classrooms children's work sometimes has to be put aside and taken out later when there is sufficient time to look and describe.

Over a period of almost a century then, the meaning of children's art has been expanded, its value established, through the thinking, research, and practice of psychologists, philosophers, educators, and artists. The ways of looking at children's art that follow draw from all of these precedents.

6

Observing Children's Art: Two Perspectives

Two distinct but intersecting perspectives on child art—two kinds of interest in it—are implicit in the foregoing. Both perspectives are useful.

The first perspective emphasizes the specific qualities of a piece of work (or body of work)—its special, idiosyncratic, and revealing character that sheds light on a child's particular ways of engaging with the world—pointing up his or her consistent style and persistent themes over time. Art is seen as communication as well as self-expression, a means for the individual (or group) to find a unique voice, to make himself or herself (themselves) known. Considerations here are primarily aesthetic and appreciative. This perspective has been particularly enriched by the work of Dewey, Freud, Read, Winnicott, and Carini.

The second perspective puts more emphasis on commonalities—how the qualities of particular works by children can be generalized to the work of all children. It views child art as a manifestation of visual thinking and considers how art formulates (represents and further develops) conceptual understanding and how, over time, children's ongoing work gives evidence to this understanding. The focus here is on aspects of symbolic representation, the gradual progress toward representing "the appearance of things" according to the conventions of the surrounding culture. Considerations include scale, perspective and dimensionality, metonymy (a part standing for the whole), selectivity, composition, expressiveness, and other aspects of realism. The individual's development is related to a

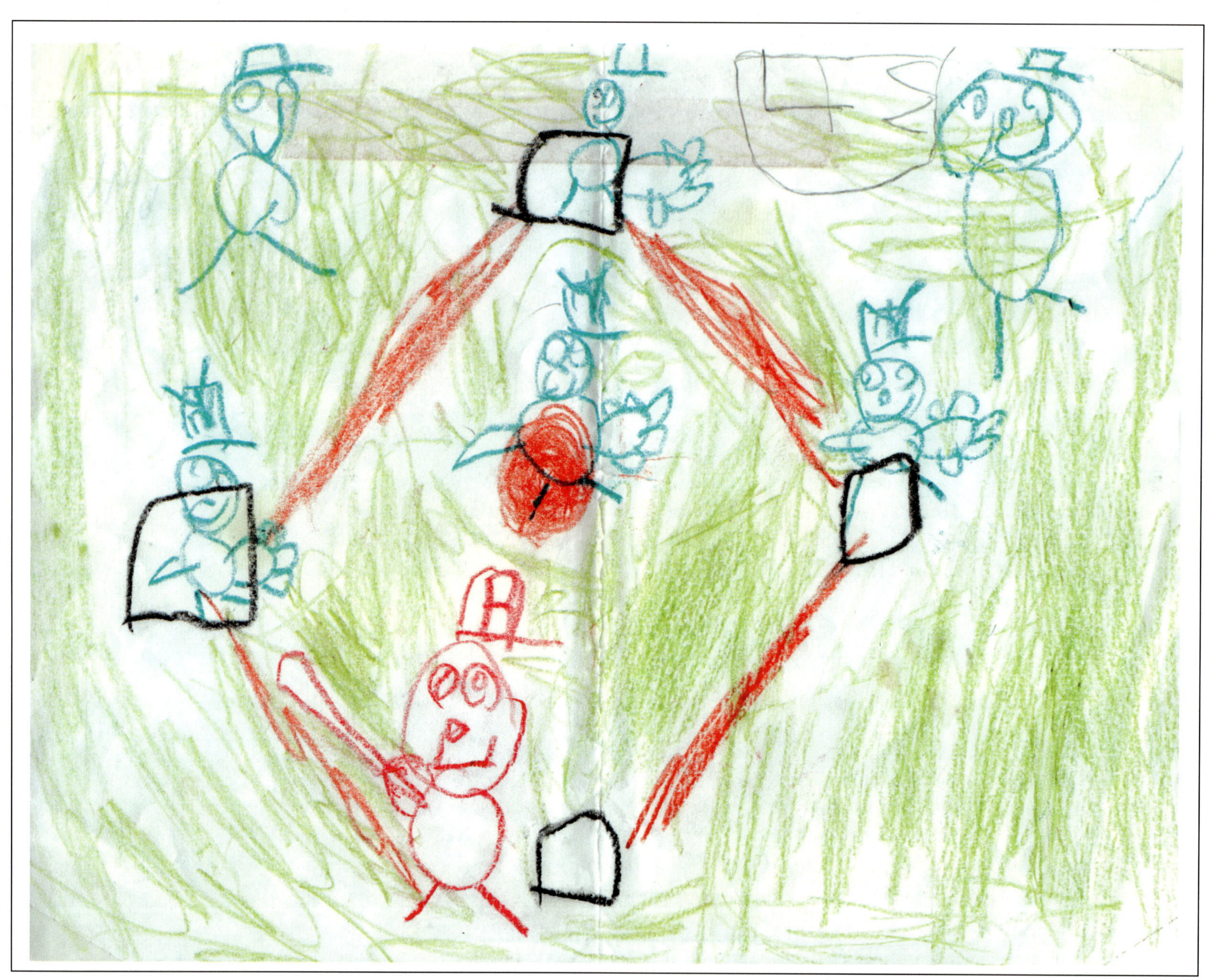

A baseball game by Allan, age 6.

continuum derived from the "ordinary" work of other children. The previously cited writings of Lowenfeld, Arnheim, and Gardner, although by no means confined to these considerations, are particularly relevant here.[13]

Both perspectives require "dwelling" in the "border area," carrying out close observations and descriptions of the artwork itself. Together they enable observers—teacher, parent, or other interested persons—to begin to "see into," understand, and appreciate a child's drawing or painting and to put their responses into words.

Example: Allan's baseball picture

Allan, like other children, explored his interests and extended his understanding through art. One of his interests was baseball, and he was learning to be both a player and observer of the game.

Perspective one: Descriptive characteristics

The easiest, most natural way of describing a piece of work is to begin with the obvious and literal and to progress toward the more subtle and interpretive. Beginning with the literal, although it may at first seem simplistic, requires us to "see" the object, to look with care before reacting. Group reflections on children's work at the Prospect School (Carini 1982) ordinarily followed this course, from the obvious to the suggested.

Six questions provide a useful guide to description (see the chart on page 32). In order to make the meaning of the procedure clear, responses to each question are given, first from observation of a drawing by Allan and then of a painting by Adam. Each child was 6 years old at the time their pictures were done.

1. ***Materials, context: What is it made of? And, if the information is available, when and under what circumstances was it made?***

Allan's drawing was made with crayons on an 8½-by-11-inch sheet of white typing paper. The numbers in the box at the upper right were written in pencil. The drawing was done at home on the kitchen table while Allan was waiting for supper. It was one of many he did on the same subject.

2. ***Basic elements, techniques: What can the observer see?***

A diamond drawn in orange, a black square at each of the angles; seven figures drawn with lines, six of them turquoise blue, the seventh red. Each of the figures has a circular head with facial features: two circular eyes, some with inner circles suggesting pupils. All of the figures have mouths like half moons, curving up at each side—except the one in red at the bottom of the diamond whose mouth is more angular, consisting of three straight lines. All of the figures except two, the ones in the upper left and upper middle, have noses drawn as circles or dots. Each figure has a circle for a body and a pair of straight stick legs. (Two figures, upper left and upper right, lack arms.) The figure at the top of the diamond has what appears to be a hand covered by a mitt, the mitt drawn as a circle with five bumps or semicircles along the edge. The three figures on the middle level have such a mitt attached to one side of the body and a more-or-less triangular shape (arm?) on the other. Each figure also wears a cap—a square (or in the case of the red figure, a half-round) over a horizontal line—some of the caps touching, some slightly above, the circular heads. The figure in red has two curved lines (arms?) coming out of the left (his right) side of the circular body, holding a bat. There is a circular, scribbled orange shape in the center of the diamond, partially overlapping the middle figure. The background is colored in with olive green crayon, the lines going different directions, some of them overlapping the figures (upper right and upper left); two numbers—a 4 and what appears to be a backwards 3—inside a box at the upper right are drawn in pencil. (Question marks in this description indicate possible unwarranted assumptions.)

Descriptive Characteristics in Considering a Child's Artwork

What is it made of? In what context?	*What can the observer see?*	*What does it represent?*	*How is it organized?*	*What is it about?*	*Where does the idea come from?*
Materials/context, such as:	**Basic elements/ techniques, such as:**	**Character of communication, such as:**	**Aspects of organization/meaning, such as:**	**Function/intent, such as:**	**Sources/origin, such as:**
size tools medium at home on a school trip in class	lines/angles shapes symmetry colors/values overlaps	design story scene symbol	perspective composition action point of view completion	providing information explaining/investigating expressing feelings entertaining/amusing narrating/recalling experimenting exploring ideas	imagination observation literature imitation TV conversation assignments "messing about"

3. *Character of communication: What does it represent?*

Allan's picture evidently represents a baseball game in progress between the Boston Red Sox (figure in red with *B* on cap) and the New York Yankees (in blue with *NY* on caps). The Red Sox are at bat, the Yankees in the field. Black squares indicate the bases. The circular orange scribble in the middle of the diamond probably represents the pitcher's mound. The paths between bases are outlined by orange, scribbly lines. The grass in and around the diamond is olive green. Part of the story is indicated by the score inside the penciled square at the upper right: four to three.

The batter (although facing the viewer) is waiting for the ball to be pitched. The outfielders are ready for the play. (Three of the usual players are missing from the Yankee team: catcher, shortstop, center fielder.)

4. *Aspects of organization, meaning: How is the picture organized?*

The composition of the picture is controlled by the shape of the diamond itself, the figures disposed both inside and around it in near-symmetry. There is the slightest suggestion of perspective in the relative sizes of the batter and second baseman—although this is contradicted by the large size of both left and right fielders. All of the figures are facing front, even the batter, whom one might expect to see from the back. Certain significant details are emphasized: the baseball caps with insignia, mitts, and facial features of players. The pitcher's mound (if that is what is represented) is particularly vivid—the only filled-in shape, placed right at the center of the paper. The bases, too, are emphasized, drawn sharply with heavy black lines superimposed on the figures of the three basemen. The players are drawn entirely in line, in the color of team to which they belong.

From the way the colors are superimposed, it looks as though the figures were drawn first, then the grass, the orange diamond and ball (or mound) next, and finally the four square bases. The scoreboard may have been added at the end.

5. *Function, intent: What is it about?*

This drawing demonstrates keen interest in, and knowledge about, the game of baseball. The disposition of the players, the depiction of their equipment and attributes—all show a confident grasp of the game's structure as well as considerable concrete information. The fact that three players are missing from the Yankees' team does not make us lose confidence in Allan's control of the facts: he left out figures that were not easy to fit in (outfielders whose stations would have been beyond the scope of the drawing as delimited by Allan) and that would have confused the clarity of the composition and "story." We can feel fairly sure that Allan knows there are three outfielders, a shortstop, and certainly a catcher (a conspicuous presence in any baseball game) on each team. Allan's feeling about the game is conveyed by the intensity of the scene, the air of expectation—the prominent bases outlined in black and the front-facing batter holding up his bat—a moment when something is about to happen.

6. *Sources, origin: Where does the idea come from?*

Judging from the kinds of details Allan supplies and the overall composition of the drawing, one might assume its inspiration was Allan's interest in the game. He is representing, as well as he can, given the limits of the materials, his understanding of the formal, rule-bound ritual called baseball. Sources of information might have been TV, conversations with friends, his own experiences playing baseball and perhaps attending games at Fenway Park. The scene, although imagined, seems based on observation and experience.

We can assume by now a close familiarity on the part of the observer with Allan's drawing. In turning then to the second perspective, we will take a step away, so to speak, in order to see Allan's drawing related to the ordinary work of other children rather than solely as the unique expression of one child's sensibility. The drawing, of course, is unmistakably Allan's; at the same time it will seem to the experienced eye of a teacher quite familiar, even typical of 6-year-old boys. This kind of double view should enrich how we see child art.

Perspective two: Developmental continuum

From how and where it was done, we know that Allan's drawing is spontaneous, original work—that is, not the result of an assignment, not corrected, not copied from a model. Allan, at a particular period in his life and limited by the materials at hand, was working out and recording his understanding of the game of baseball: its essence, how he perceived it, what it was to him. He undoubtedly knew more about the game than he tells in this picture; the picture represents his stripped-down sense of its meaning as he was able to convey it with crayons on a two-dimensional sheet of paper, 8½ by 11 inches.

His drawing offers us an opportunity to see where Allan is developmentally (see the chart on page 35): the level of his perceptions, use of symbolization, and control over the conventions and techniques involved in translating a three-dimensional event into a small, two-dimensional image.

1. *Symbolization: What are the elements in the picture that have built-in significance for an observer who shares with Allan a common culture?*

Not yet under the constraints of realism, Allan feels free to represent only what matters to him, the important aspects of the game. These are emphasized through certain details, already described, that carry more than an ordinary

Developmental Continuum in Children's Drawings

Preschool (ages 2–5)

- scribbles, loops, zigzags, wavy lines, jabs, arcs—often partially off the paper at first
- chance forms or shapes
- trying out different effects
- meaning in the act itself, not in results or product
- experimenting with leaving a mark, with colors and motions to leave a sign or have an effect
- reflecting motion of hand/arm
- separate lines, circlelike shapes, combined straight and curved lines
- other basic forms, controlled marks, first schematic formulae, mandalalike shapes

Sources: physical act of moving a hand and arm, basic concepts such as the circle, exploration of possibilities of line

Early primary (ages 4–6)

- shapes combined, becoming schemas; intentional image repetition of schemas; development of preferred schemas
- beginnings of representation, often of people; letterlike forms; basic forms represented consistently—houses, flowers, boats, people; animals in profile
- meaning (subject matter) increasingly readable
- repertory or symbolic forms repeated, practiced, and new elements added
- beginnings of individual style (e.g., typical way of drawing a house)
- figures isolated, no context or baseline; each discrete (no overlapping of whole or of parts); size and details according to perceived importance or interest (e.g., long arms)
- several figures on the page; beginning representing of events or narratives; schematic figures placed in a larger concept, for example, knowing an elephant is a four-legged animal with a trunk, the child uses a well-established routine, or schema, for drawing animals—cats, dogs, and so forth—and adds a trunk

Sources: child's concepts and knowledge about the world, which take precedence over direct perception (as in the elephant example above)

Middle primary (ages 5–8)

- elaboration and variation of schematic figures and experimentation; repetition of imagery, practicing "set pictures" (always drawn the same way), such as racing cars
- details often traditional or formulaic, such as windows with tie-back curtains, chimneys with smoke coming out at an angle, girls defined by skirts and long hair
- narrative, illustrative, inventive; baselines often multiple; "see-through" houses; most figures in own space, without overlapping

Sources: copying conventional renderings by other children, imagination, book illustrations, TV, cartoons, and so on

Late primary (ages 7–10)

- increased differentiation—of kinds of animals, flowers, buildings, and so on; practiced drawing of favorite subjects—battle scenes, princesses, characters from TV, comics, books; pictures often telling detailed stories
- interest in drawing from nature
- figures sometimes in profile, with limbs bent, props added to indicate roles (e.g., cowboy hat and rope); increasing demand for looking real
- color more naturalistic; scenery, overlapping, shadows, beginning perspective, and shading; more realistic use of scale; distance, elevations, and perspective added
- backgrounds: landscapes, seascapes, sky, underground, under the sea; figures more logically interrelated; elevations, consistent viewpoints given
- action: eye still seeing one relationship at a time, the mind having to put them together on the page to solve problems; fine control of line

Sources: observation, imagination, book knowledge, copying, and so forth

> *Not yet under the constraint of realism, young children feel free to represent in their art only what matters to them.*

share of meaning. Perhaps the most basic fact is that there are two teams. Allan represents this fact quite simply by drawing the Yankees in blue, the Red Sox batter in red—not just their outfits, but each entire figure. The diamond itself, which for adults as well can stand for the game of baseball (Joe DiMaggio was a hero of "the diamond"), has been gone over several times with an orange crayon, emphasizing its centrality to the structure of the game. The human figures who might otherwise have represented any ordinary persons—with eyes, noses, mouths, round heads, round bodies, stick legs—become baseball players by virtue of two distinguishing features: caps with team insignia and mitts. The large bat held at a slant identifies the figure in red as the batter.

These are, to be sure, real things, real elements of the game that Allan has drawn. But the attention given to them (as well as what has been omitted) adds meaning: the baseball cap with a large, red *B* on it signifies more than just a baseball cap with a letter of the alphabet on it; it specifically identifies a member of the Red Sox team and, thus, an opponent of the men in blue.

An infinite number of elements that might have been included, of course, are left out: not only the team's three additional players, but also the audience, bleachers, flying planes overhead, ads, paper cups, TV screen, bullpen, player uniforms with letters and numbers on the shirts, arms and mitts for the left and right fielders, umpires, coaches, dugout with other team members, the baseball itself, and so on. But what Allan has included is sufficient for his purposes: to express and communicate his sense of the game.

2. *Elements of realism: How and to what extent does the drawing convey perspective and viewpoint, scale, shading, overlapping, background?*

Allan is apparently not yet interested in creating an illusion of reality, of approximating as closely as possible the appearance of things. The figures of the players are drawn conventionally and minimally, with only the necessary attributes. Allan has a certain way of drawing the human figure, a shorthand method. His players are differentiated, not from each other but from most people, by three attributes: cap, mitt, and bat. Art educator Nancy Smith, echoing Arnheim, wrote that children first depict "their conception of the largest category to which the object belongs . . . later in this phase, having established symbols for basic types of objects, children move on to depicting 'subcategories' . . . by adding more attributes to their basic symbols" (1983, 8). In the case of Allan's drawing, the category would be people and the subcategory, baseball players.

There is no consistent suggestion of scale or perspective. The size of the players is not strictly related to their nearness to the viewer. Although the batter might seem to be in the foreground by virtue of his size, the right fielder is equally large. The size of the batter, in fact, may be due more to his importance in the drama than to his position on the field. The batter, of course, faces us. Why? One can only speculate that Allan either wasn't interested in drawing someone from the back, didn't know how to draw someone from the back, or simply preferred to show the Red Sox batter's features and pose from the more familiar frontal view.[14] In any case, scale and perspective do not operate as constraints on Allan's perception of the game.

The figures of the players are discrete, each in his own position with no overlapping. Bases and the pitcher's mound are superimposed in an expressive rather than realistic way. (Perhaps Allan simply realized, after finishing the picture, that he had left out an important element, the bases, which he then drew in at the appropriate places—apparently not bothered by the fact that they were on top of (rather than behind) the players.

Although there are no baselines as such, except literally the lines between bases (a different meaning of the word), there is a suggestion of background, of scene: grass, diamond, and bases. The elements of the drawing are related to each other within a larger context, that of the game.

3. *Expression and communication: Does the work express feeling and communicate content?*

One might say that Allan's drawing communicates a good deal of knowledge about baseball—the disposition of the players, the two opposing teams, the shape of the diamond, and, by implication, the definition of a run; also the score posted at the upper right. The drawing is more about information than feeling. Although it conveys an air of expectation and even tension—the batter appearing distinctly anxious—the drawing seems more focused on content than on feeling. Action, too, is implied rather than depicted. The scene, which seems suspended in time, is essentially diagrammatic.

Although this analysis is of some length, about a basically unexceptional and relatively simple example of child art, not everything there is to say has been said about it by any means. A careful observer could add to both the description and interpretation, while still staying within the compass of the work itself, that is, without speculating on the child's psychological makeup, potential for learning, home situation, or other presumed influences on the work—the kinds of intrusions specifically cautioned against by Patricia Carini (1982). Such speculation is neither respectful nor necessary outside of explicitly therapeutic situations. As the preceding descriptions demonstrate, much can be said while staying with the work itself.

These same approaches will be used to comment on the second example, a painting of a giraffe in the zoo done in school by a first-grade boy.

Example: Adam's giraffe painting

Adam had either visited the zoo or learned about zoos through TV or books. He left this painting behind in the classroom where he made it. Perhaps the process of painting itself was what interested him, not the final product.

PERSPECTIVE ONE: Descriptive characteristics

1. ***Materials, context: What is it made of? When and under what circumstances was it made?***

Painted in tempera on manila paper, 8½ by 11 inches, the work has three lines of green-and-white composition paper taped to the bottom. Adam, the painter, is a first grader in the Literacy Center of an urban public school. The center, where each primary-grade class spends a 40-minute period twice a week, contains many books and a variety of art materials. The period usually begins with a group, shared reading; then children choose an activity. The more particular circumstances under which the giraffe painting was done are not known.

2. ***Basic elements, techniques: What can the observer see?***

The main element is an orange shape representing a giraffe. (Although staying with literal description here, we can't pretend that we don't recognize as such, the giraffe, tree, cage, ground, and sky.) The giraffe has a small, triangular black mark (eye) near the top of his head. To the giraffe's right is a small, dark brown tree with vertical trunk, five branches slanting up on each side. Each branch has a patch of green leaves superimposed. The branches are more spaced out and start lower down on the right side.

Seven horizontal and seven vertical bars painted with thick black strokes are partially obscured by the giraffe and tree. At the bottom of the picture is a band of horizontal green grass with, toward the left, small bits of orange and yellow superimposed. A strip of blue sky crosses the top of the paper, fairly even in width except where it is interrupted by the top of the giraffe's head. The remainder of the paper is unpainted.

The figure of the giraffe is slightly elevated from the green baseline; the tree trunk touches it. While the blue and green strips border the top and bottom of the paper, the giraffe, bars, and tree occupy roughly the right-hand two-thirds of the picture space. The painter's name

A giraffe in the zoo by Adam, age 6.

For young children, animals are recognized, virtually represented, by their distinguishing characteristics: elephants by their trunks, crocodiles by their teeth, and giraffes by their long necks.

appears in the space between sky and grass in the left-hand third of the picture.

The orange-and-black painted areas are fairly opaque, although the colors intermingle in places, the black showing through on the giraffe's lower neck and at the bottom of its legs. The orange is superimposed over the black cage bars, obscuring parts of both the vertical and horizontal bars. The tree trunk is painted with a mixture of black and brown that is also superimposed over both the bars and the green ground. The green patches (leaves), in turn, are painted over the brown–black branches, and the yellowish green ground line seems to have been painted over black, which shows through at the edges of the strokes.

From these overlaps and superimpositions, it appears that the cage was probably painted first, then the grass, the tree, the giraffe, and finally the sky, which carefully skirts around the top of the giraffe's head. The black bars are painted with strong brushstrokes, though four of them look slightly broken just to the right of the giraffe's front leg. The giraffe's outlines are somewhat wavery, and the leaves splotchy. The ground and sky are painted with strong horizontal strokes. The yellow and red dots on the grass to the left are done with the end of the brush and/or possibly dripped. There are basically five colors (although some are a bit intermixed): orange, black, brown, green, and blue.

Adam has attached ten words of explanation in invented spelling at the bottom of his painting, "AG Rf eS eteN Levz aNd heS eN the zoo." Translated into conventional spelling, the story reads "A giraffe is eating leaves and he's in the zoo."

3. *Character of the communication: What does it represent?*

Even without the painter's explanation, we would have understood the subject of the painting with no difficulty. Just as the written words constitute a complete sentence, the painting makes a complete statement, leaving little room for ambiguity.

For young children, animals are recognized, virtually represented, by their distinguishing characteristics: elephants by their trunks, tigers by their stripes, crocodiles by their teeth, and giraffes by their long necks—and the main thing about the giraffe's long neck is that it enables him to eat leaves off the top of trees. This describes the giraffe in the painting: he has an outsized neck and is eating the uppermost leaves on the left side of the tree. One can even detect small lines probably representing his mouth and tongue. The giraffe's impressive height is emphasized by his head sticking up above the cage and actually reaching into the sky.

Another bit of supportive evidence about what the painter sees as important is the order of the sentence below the painting.

Ordinarily one would expect the second part to come first to set the scene: "The giraffe is in the zoo"—or even, "This is a giraffe and he's in the zoo." Adam, however, has begun with "A giraffe is eating leaves" and then explains that "he's in the zoo."

The giraffe is simply, almost minimally, depicted (no pattern on his hide, for example). The only embellishments are the flowers on the grass and, in a sense, the painter's name on the left. The colors are true to life with the possible exception of the giraffe himself, who is a brighter orange than most giraffes. Each element in the painting is simply and clearly stated: sky, cage, tree, giraffe, grass. The whole represents a zoo scene: main character and setting.

4. *Aspects of organization, meaning: How is the picture organized?*

The painting has a single baseline of green grass at the bottom and line of blue sky at the top, each of these discrete and conventional except where the sky is pierced by the head of the giraffe. The elements in the scene are viewed in elevation, the peculiarity of the viewpoint being that the cage is behind rather than in front of the giraffe. Thus, the observer is on the same side of the bars as the giraffe—inside the cage.

The giraffe appears almost like a cutout, in profile with only two legs and one eye visible. The tree is also essentially two-dimensional, the branches emerging from either side of the vertical trunk, although the mixture of brown and black paint creates some illusion of three-dimensionality. Slight depth of setting is conveyed by the cage appearing behind and, thus, slightly further away from the observer than the giraffe or tree.

As remarked above, the main content of the painting occupies the right-hand two-thirds of the paper. Lateral balance, however, is to some degree maintained by the sky, grass, and the words at the bottom—all of which run the full width of the paper—and the emphases given to the left side by the painter's name and the vivid spots of color on the grass at the bottom. The giraffe/tree part of the composition is held together by the strong patternlike black bars of the cage. The lines of grass and sky provide top and bottom framing.

5. *Function/intent: What is it about?*

The scene of the giraffe in the zoo is peaceful, the feeling benign. The giraffe is a pleasant, even lovable creature with almost a stuffed-animal appearance—big, soft, and fuzzy-looking, anything but threatening. Rather delicately he is eating leaves off a tree. The cage, however, with its stern black bars, conveys a different, slightly sinister note. Although the giraffe looks content, the heavy black lines behind him indicate that he is, in fact, not free but confined with the tree in a

Within the limitations of the materials and individual knowledge and physical coordination, children are able to successfully express what they mean; in fact, the very limitations, the forced economy of means, may partly account for the inventiveness and the direct, vivid communication of children's art.

rather small space. His head up in the sky, however, conveys a sense of his being "above it all," superior to his present circumstances, dignified, and somewhat oblivious. The single eye seems to be looking inward.

We, as observers, are not only literally but also sympathetically on the giraffe's side, our feelings with him. The painting would have a very different effect if we were looking at the animal through bars. We might feel sorry for his imprisonment but would not share with him the same sense of intimacy.

There's an important point that needs to be made here: the ideas and feelings recorded above as possible responses to Adam's giraffe painting were not necessarily those of the 6-year-old painter himself when he created his picture. We don't know if Adam intended to convey the caged giraffe as sympathetic or noble. We do not even have the clues of what Adam might have said while painting the giraffe. The sense of the giraffe as sympathetic and benignly present represents an adult response informed by an individual's knowledge and experience. As in the case of every piece of visual art, the viewer and the artist both have a relationship to the work, an interpretation. Only one of these, that of the viewer, has been described. The work itself provides a common ground where meaning is expressed and from which meaning is derived. Although the two interpretations are not identical because of the differences in character and experience between artist and viewer, they inevitably overlap because of commonalities of culture and experience. Thus the object itself, the painting, accommodates to some extent the feelings, understanding, and experience of both creator and viewer. The viewer, consequently, is unlikely to radically misunderstand the painter's meaning—to see the giraffe, for example, as threatening or the scene as stormy.

6. ***Sources, origin: Where does the idea come from?***

We can't know the answer to this. Adam might have visited the zoo, but the idea could have come just as well from books or television. In any event, finally, it is the painter's feelings for the giraffe, along with his knowledge of the giraffe's form and eating habits, that inform the painting.

Perspective two: Developmental continuum

What can we say about Adam's conceptual development, his understanding of the world, from his painting of the giraffe in the zoo? A good deal, of course, could be said about his literacy skill, from the caption below the painting, among other things that he has a good sense of phonics, judging by the invented spelling; has clear, legible handwriting; writes a complete sentence; and is able to present the important information in a succinct way. In the painting we see some similar qualities: Adam's ability to use the medium, select and represent the key elements of the scene, and make a complete visual statement.

1. *Symbolization.*
Adam's painting, in fact, exemplifies one of the descriptors of art in the early primary phase (see chart on page 35): "child's concepts and knowledge about the world, which take precedence over direct perception." As we've noted, what is important about the giraffe is his long neck that reaches into the sky, enabling him to eat leaves off the top of the tree. Adam's painting, more than anything else, is an illustration of this interesting fact.

2. *Elements of realism.*
Young children commonly depict each figure in its own space, discrete and complete. They often go to some pains to avoid overlaps. Adam is still basically depicting the elements in the painting as separate entities in this way: giraffe, tree, ground, sky. The sky, although accommodating the giraffe's head, is still conceived as "up there," across the top of the paper. There's a space between sky and ground, the space where the action takes place, here as in most pictures by young children.

The flatness of the renderings, too—the giraffe seen in profile, the tree made two-dimensional—is characteristic of work by children in this developmental range. There are no shadows and no shading. In addition to integrity of shape, each major element has its assigned color (even though some of the colors appear mixed, as noted above): orange giraffe, brown tree, green leaves, black cage, blue sky, and green grass. The colors are realistic (grass is green, sky is blue).

To some extent Adam moved beyond the limitations of two-dimensionality in order to create a setting, the zoo. The giraffe and tree are in an implied three-dimensional space, because the bars are behind them. The individual entities are related—become a composition rather than a collection—by the pattern of the bars, the top and bottom framing (sky and grass), and the overlap of the giraffe with the tree (eating leaves).

Although the painting depicts an action (giraffe eating), it is essentially motionless, static. The figure of the giraffe is stationary, the body composed of three vertical blocks (legs and neck) and two horizontal blocks (body and head). The schematic tree is stiff: vertical trunk, straight branches angling out at either side. The bars of the cage are straight verticals and horizontals. The grass and sky are horizontal stripes. Except for the slanting branches, the world is conceived in perpendiculars. The fuzzy outlines of the giraffe and the splotchy leaves and flowers soften the angular effect.

3. *Expression and communication.*
Adam's painting illustrates how, within the limitations of the materials and children's own knowledge and physical coordination,

they are able to successfully express what they mean. In fact, the very limitations, the enforced economy of means, may partly be responsible for children's inventiveness that results in direct, vivid, communicative art. Like adult artists, they have to solve the basic problems of the medium and make choices yet without some of the constraints encountered later on. For example, Adam solved the conflict over space between the giraffe's head and the line of sky by having the sky stop on one side and start up again on the other. The effect, although not realistic, works. We get the idea—that the giraffe's head is very high.

Because of his feeling for the giraffe and, presumably, his wish to show the giraffe in his entirety, yet also a wish to show that he's in the zoo, Adam superimposes the painting of the giraffe over the bars rather than vice versa (the usual animal-in-cage image). Here again he achieves his purposes. If Adam had been constrained by a more sophisticated knowledge of perspective, he might have been obliged to sacrifice some of his intended meaning—if he realized, for example, that he was painting the giraffe from the viewpoint of someone in there with him, he might have had second thoughts. Paul Klee struggled against this kind of sacrifice of essential meaning as he intentionally unlearned the rules of realistic representation that Adam, perhaps less conflicted at age 6, still has to learn.

Another example of how Adam subordinates reality to his purposes is the size of the tree: he makes the tree unusually small to enable the giraffe to eat from its top. If the tree were the size an ordinary tree would be relative to the height of the cage, the giraffe's head would have to project beyond the upper edge of the paper.

In sum, the painting of the giraffe characterizes the thinking, interests, and feelings of one 6-year-old boy, Adam. It is his work, and its relationship to other work by the same child might be apparent to Adam's teacher, parent, or good friend. At the same time the painting shows Adam dealing with many of the problems inherent in both understanding and representing the three-dimensional world in two dimensions, problems also being dealt with by his peers: color, viewpoint, overlaps, scale, action, setting, and so on. As children gain in experience and knowledge of the world, their ways of representing that world change and develop. Yet there are threads of continuity—subtle yet perceptible preoccupations and characteristic elements of style—that endure and remain visible in their creative work.

7

Summary Descriptions

What, then, are the practical implications of the above exercises in observation? Clearly, each teacher can't go through a similar process with each piece of work by each child. The questions I've outlined should be taken as suggestions for looking, ways to begin seeing what is there and what might be said about it. An observer doesn't need to attend to all of the suggested questions in any one instance. Nonetheless, practice with this kind of close description will eventually enable a teacher, parent, or other interested person to see more easily into a picture—and not feel the need to fill in awkward silences with quick judgments or critical statements. Whether judgments are positive or negative, they tend to be summary and to close out further perceptions and thoughtful responses.

After looking at a piece of work and noting down responses to some of the guiding questions, the observer should be able to write a concise, accurate, meaningful, and basically descriptive paragraph about either one piece of work or a series of pieces collected over time.

This kind of observation can also be carried out as a group process, with each person in turn adding to the description of the work. One person can be assigned as recorder, responsible for noting individual comments and then summarizing them at the end of the discussion. Individual perceptions will often trigger the insights of others in a group, the sum in terms of understanding adding up to more than the parts. Such a process can be institutionalized as a regular form of staff development—one to which each person can be an equally informed contributor.

Summary of Allan's picture

The paragraph that follows represents a distillation of the description of Allan's baseball drawing. Some of the characteristics previously noted have been synthesized in order to make a brief statement, suitable for a report sent home, a parent conference, or for a teacher's own records.

Allan's drawing of a game between the Boston Red Sox and New York Yankees shows his firm grasp of the structure of the game itself through the accurate detail and overall design. In his drawing, Allan ably organizes and translates to paper a complex event. The picture is clear and readable, with no unnecessary or extraneous elements. Allan makes use of significant detail to convey the meaning of the scene he has drawn: caps with insignia, color of members of opposing teams, diagram of field, and so forth. Although not yet concerned with some aspects of realism (such as perspective and scale), Allan conveys an entire scene with the main actors (or players) logically interrelated.

The characteristics of an individual child's work often will appear over time as recurrent qualities and themes, not perhaps identifiable in advance but recognizable in retrospect.

The above commentary stays, on the whole, with the descriptive rather than the judgmental. It pertains to the drawing itself, putting on record particular qualities of Allan's work that can be appreciated and kept track of over time. Two perspectives are brought to bear: the drawing as it expresses the quality of Allan's intense interest in baseball and as it illustrates Allan's exploration of the structure of the game and solutions to the difficult problem of translating from the three-dimensional world to two-dimensional paper. In practice, the two perspectives (descriptive characteristics and developmental continuum) are closely interrelated; they cannot be wholly separated, nor need they be. Their usefulness to the observer is in providing for appreciation of the peculiar style of an individual's work and recognition of how that work is related to the work of others. With experience on the part of the observer, the two perspectives will come together as one.

Summary of Adam's painting

A summary view of Adam's painting offers descriptive and developmental comment.

The painting shows Adam's ability to make a clear, simple statement with brush, paper, and paint, echoing the clarity of his sentence of explanation attached at the bottom. His subject is a giraffe in the zoo. The impressive thing about giraffes—the feature that distinguishes them from other animals—is the length of their necks. Adam emphasizes this notable feature by having his giraffe eating leaves from the top of a tree, his head literally in the sky.

The colors Adam uses are true to life although without modulations (shading). The main elements (tree and giraffe) are conceived as discrete entities (i.e., each in its own space), the cage appearing behind both. Not yet concerned with realistic effects, Adam solves logical conflicts in favor of meaning: the tree is small enough for the giraffe to eat leaves from the top; the sky parts to make way for the giraffe's head; the cage is behind the giraffe, allowing him to be fully seen.

The basically separate elements (sky, grass, tree, giraffe), flat figures, and essentially two-dimensional space are characteristics of early primary art. Adam, however, is also trying out ideas to do with depth and three-dimensionality that show, perhaps, a new kind of awareness: the cage behind the giraffe and tree, the leaves painted over the branches, the giraffe's mouth overlapping the tree. We might expect Adam to experiment soon in his artwork with three-dimensional representation.

Year-end comments

The same ways of looking can be applied to collections of children's work, kept (and dated) over a period of time, with attention to both descriptive characteristics and development. The paragraph that follows comments on Allan's work over one academic year.

This year Allan's drawing was a way for him to explore and consolidate his expanding understanding of aspects of his experience. In the fall he drew and painted mainly his own family—mother and father, baby sister, dog, house. These elements were usually lined up horizontally across the page with no background or baselines indicated. Female figures were distinguished by the conventional triangular skirt and long hair. (Note: His mother has short hair and often wears trousers.) By January Allan had extended his subject matter to include himself and his mother in the playground, a huge and possibly scary slide represented by two parallel lines crossing the paper from upper left to lower right; a car with faces appearing in the windows; two people—one much larger than the other—with a ball; and several paintings of dinosaurs copied from a book.

In April Allan began a series of baseball pictures, at the same time changing his preferred medium from paint to markers—perhaps in order to record significant details with more accuracy and control. The first few of these drawings depicted players wearing caps, some holding bats. Soon after, Allan began to draw whole scenes, relating the figures to each other within a meaningful context—the baseball diamond. He was still drawing the schematic figures he had developed during his period of family pictures earlier on. Separate identities were indicated through the use of selective symbols: letter *B*, for example, on the cap of the Boston Red Sox player. Allan's drawings at this stage focus more on content or information than on mood or feeling. His art is beginning to move from the early primary to middle primary stage of development (see the chart on page 35)—the figures are schematic, no attempt made at realistic effects but clearly showing the beginnings of scene and narrative.

Some of the characteristics of an individual child's work will appear over time as recurrent qualities and themes, not perhaps identifiable in advance but recognizable in retrospect. In Allan's case they might include an interest in sports, the diagrammatic clarity of his rendering, his accuracy and attention to detail, the exploration of symmetry or other geometric forms; for Adam, feelings of empathy, quality of directness of expression, possibly even a continuing interest in animals. One might also see a certain quality of shape, line, pattern, and composition, already evident in Adam's giraffe picture, echoed in future work. These subtle but distinct consistencies are impossible to predict or identify in advance, but are recognizable in retrospect. Characteristics recur in different forms and contexts but retain, mysteriously, traces of the same sensibility.

Conclusion

Given an optimal situation—a school in which art is fully validated and supported in the primary grades—children will produce work that both evidences and furthers their understanding of the world, art that expresses the self and at the same time develops the self. As an activity, art is central to children's emotional and intellectual development; as product, artworks provide a valuable record of each child's growth and unique way of relating to the world and of the qualities of mind and disposition that endure and constitute the fabric of individual identity.

Philosophers, psychologists, educators, and artists in the 20th century have enlarged our views, given us a broad basis for understanding and appreciating child art. Starting then, with a deepened sense of the potential meaning, teachers, parents, and others can learn to study children's works by dwelling in that border space between the individual and his or her surroundings where creative activity takes place. Observing the work, moving from description to insight based on a developmental continuum, recognizing the unique marks of the individual consciousness as it encounters the outside world, teachers, parents, researchers, and friends can become constructive and articulate appreciators of child art. Art then will regain its logical place, a place of central importance in learning.

Notes

1. Over the last three decades, writing, reading, speaking, and listening have all been recognized as aspects of literacy. Writing has consequently assumed an important place in the curriculum in many, although not all, school districts. See the work of Donald Graves, Lucy M. Calkins, Nancie Atkins, Marie Clay, Kenneth and Yetta Goodman, Don Holdaway, Constance Weaver, and Jerome Harste, among many others.
2. For example, the cover of an 1854 instructional manual by Rembrandt Peale, carried the lengthy title *Graphics, the Art of Accurate Delineation, a System of School Exercise, for the Education of the Eye and the Training of the Hand as Auxiliary to Writing, Geography and Drawing,* reproduced in Wygant (1983, 20).
3. Lawrence Cremin, in his monumental history of American education, wrote, "Hall made child study a national movement, with Clark University [Worcester, Massachusetts] as its headquarters, the *Pedagogical Seminary* as its messenger, and a network of women as its driving force." See his *American Education: The Metropolitan Experience, 1876–1980* (New York: Harper & Row, 1988), 279. Hart edited the *Pedagogical Seminary,* 1891–1924.
4. Many schools since the 1920s, in large part independent schools, have used children's work as a key to curriculum planning. One of the most notable was the Prospect School in North Bennington, Vermont. Methods developed at this small, progressive school are discussed later on in this book.
5. Having attended a progressive elementary school myself in the early 1930s, the Windward School in White Plains, New York, I can attest to the centrality of art and crafts in the life of the school. I have vivid memories not only of children's work displayed almost literally everywhere but a strong residual sense of the respect with which it was regarded by teachers and parents. The creative impulse, in general, was encouraged and valued in the progressive schools. As an adult, I retain a feeling of possibility that, with a little help or instruction, I can undertake to *make* almost anything that can be made of common materials, such as wood, clay, or fabric.

6. Burt later became well known for his falsification of research data on IQs. Stephen J. Gould (1981) gives a fascinating account of how Cyril Burt, a highly respected professional, falsified data to support his own beliefs about inherited intelligence.

7. Burt's stages are described by Herbert Read, *Education Through Art,* 3rd ed. (New York: Pantheon, [1943] 1956), 118–19.

8. In *Education Through Art,* Read describes at length his classification system and its links to Jung's psychological types (see especially pages 140–47).

9. The Prospect School in North Bennington, Vermont, was, unhappily, forced to close in 1991 for financial reasons.

10. Group processes for looking in depth at children's work were developed by Patricia Carini and colleagues at the Prospect School. These processes, along with the theory informing them, are described in two monographs by Carini (1979, 1982). Slides of the children's artworks, copies of their writings, and related teacher observations from over a 20-year period have been put together and published as the *Reference Edition of the Prospect Archives* (1985). The publication, which includes works by 36 children (18 boys and 18 girls), is organized developmentally by child. Individual collections, some of which cover seven or eight years of schooling, are available for rental by teachers and other researchers. For information, write to The Prospect Archive, North Bennington, Vermont 05257.

11. Conversations recorded in personal observations by the author.

12. Observation by the author.

13. I have included Viktor Lowenfeld in the second group. Although he is perhaps best known for his developmental scheme, he was interested also in the social/emotional/aesthetic aspect of child art. In fact, none of the writers I've cited adhered strictly to one perspective. Almost all were interested in child art as a whole. I've chosen to emphasize those aspects of their work that are useful for my particular purposes.

14. Allan's mother discussed the baseball drawing with Allan over a year after its execution, when Allan was 7½ years old. She asked him why he had drawn the batter facing the observer instead of the pitcher. Allan's logical explanation: "I was younger then."

References

Arnheim, R. 1969. *Visual thinking.* Berkeley: University of California Press.

Arnheim, R. 1989. *Thoughts on art education.* Los Angeles, CA: Getty Center for Education in the Arts.

Burt, C. 1940. *The factors of the mind: An introduction to factor-analysis in psychology.* London: University of London Press.

Carini, P.F. 1979. *The art of seeing and the visibility of the person.* Monograph, North Dakota Study Group on Evaluation. Grand Forks: University of North Dakota.

Carini, P.F. 1982. *The school lives of seven children: A five year study.* Monograph, North Dakota Study Group on Evaluation. Grand Forks: University of North Dakota.

Cassirer, E. 1957. *The philosophy of symbolic forms.* 3 vols. New Haven, CT: Yale University Press.

Cremin, L.A. 1961. *The transformation of the school.* New York: Knopf.

Cremin, L.A. 1988. *American education: The metropolitan experience, 1876–1980.* New York: Harper & Row.

Darling-Hammond, L. 1994. Performance-based assessment and educational equity. *Harvard Educational Review* 64 (1): 5–30.

Dewey, J. 1934. *Art as experience.* New York: Capricorn.

Dix, L. 1939. *A charter for progressive education.* New York: Teachers College Press.

Ernst, K. 1994. *Picturing learning.* Portsmouth, NH: Heinemann.

Fein, S. 1974. *Heidi's horse.* Pleasant Hill, CA: Exelrod.

Fein, S. 1993. *First drawings: Genesis of visual thinking.* Pleasant Hill, CA: Exelrod.

Field, D. 1970. *Change in art education.* London: Routledge & Kegan Paul.

Gallas, K. 1992. Arts as epistemology: Enabling children to know what they know. In *Arts as education,* eds. M.R. Goldberg & A. Phillips, 19–31. Cambridge, MA: Harvard University Press.

Gardner, H. 1980. *Artful scribbles: The significance of children's drawings.* New York: Basic.

Gardner, H. 1983. *Frames of mind: The theory of multiple intelligences.* New York: Basic.

Gardner, H. 1990. *Art education and human development.* Los Angeles, CA: Getty Center for Education in the Arts.

Getty Center for Education in the Arts. 1985. *Beyond creating: The place for art in America's schools.* Los Angeles, CA: Getty Center.

Goodman, N. 1968. *Languages of art.* Indianapolis, IN: Bobbs-Merrill.

Goodnow, J. 1977. *Children drawing.* Cambridge, MA: Harvard University Press.

Gould, S.J. 1981. *The mismeasure of man.* New York: W.W. Norton.

Hein, G.E., & S. Price. 1994. *Active assessment for active science: A guide for elementary school teachers.* Portsmouth, NH: Heinemann.

Himley, M. 1991. *Shared territory: Understanding children's writing as works.* New York: Oxford University Press.

Horn, M., & J. Sieder. 1992. Looking for a Renaissance: The campaign to revise education in the arts. *U.S. News & World Report,* 30 March, 52–54.

Illsley, R. 1969. Personal communication.

Jung, C.G. [1938] 1971. *Psychological types.* Princeton, NJ: Princeton University Press.

Kellogg, R. 1969. *Analyzing children's art.* Palo Alto, CA: National Press.

Klee, P. 1964. *The diaries of Paul Klee, 1898–1918.* Berkeley: University of California Press.

Langer, S.K. 1942. *Philosophy in a new key.* Cambridge, MA: Harvard University Press.

Lindstrom, M. 1957. *Children's art.* Berkeley: University of California Press.

Lowenfeld, V. [1947], & W. L. Brittain. 1967. *Creative and mental growth.* New York: Macmillan.

Naumburg, R. 1950. *Psychoneurotic art, its function in psychotherapy.* New York: Grune & Stratton.

Olson, J.L. 1992. *Envisioning writing.* Portsmouth, NH: Heinemann.

Read, H. [1943] 1956. *Education through art.* 3rd. ed. New York: Pantheon.

Reference edition of the Prospect Archives. 1985. North Bennington, VT: Prospect Center.

Rousseau, J.J. [1780] 1948. *Emile.* New York: Dutton.

Smith, N.R. 1983. *Experience & art: Teaching children to paint.* New York: Teachers College Press.

The hundred languages of children/I cento linguaggi dei bambini. 1987. City of Reggio Emilia, Italy: Department of Education.

Winnicott, D.W. 1971. *Playing and reality.* London: Tavistock/Routledge.

Wygant, F. 1983. *Art in American schools in the nineteenth century.* Cincinnati, OH: Interwood.

Further Readings

Armstrong, M. 1980. *Closely observed children.* London: Writers & Readers Publishing.

Arnheim, R. 1954. *Art and visual perception: A psychology of the creative eye.* Berkeley: University of California Press.

Calkins, L.M. 1983. *Lessons from a child: On the teaching and learning of writing.* Portsmouth, NH: Heinemann.

Carini, P.F. 1975. *Observation and description: An alternative methodology for the investigation of human phenomena.* Monograph, North Dakota Study Group on Evaluation. Grand Forks: University of North Dakota.

Clay, M.M. 1972. *The early detection of reading difficulties.* Portsmouth, NH: Heinemann.

Clemens, S.G. 1991. Art in the classroom: Making every day special. *Young Children* 46 (2): 4–11.

Cobb, E. 1977. *The ecology of imagination in childhood.* New York: Columbia University Press.

Cole, E., & C. Schaefer. 1990. Can young children be art critics? *Young Children* 45 (2): 33–38.

DiLeo, J.H. 1983. *Interpreting children's drawings.* New York: Brunner/Mazel.

Edwards, L.C., & M.L. Nabors. 1993. The creative arts process: What it is and what it is not. *Young Children* 48 (3): 77–81.

Edwards, C., L. Gandini, & G. Forman. 1993. *The hundred languages of children: The Reggio Emilia approach to early childhood education.* Norwood, NJ: Ablex.

Feeney, S., & E. Moravcik. 1987. A thing of beauty: Aesthetic development in young children. *Young Children* 42 (6): 7–15.

Golomb, C. 1974. *Young children's sculpture and drawing: A study in representational development.* Cambridge, MA: Harvard University Press.

Goodman, Y.M, D.J. Watson, & C.L. Burke. 1987. *Reading miscue inventory: Alternative procedures.* New York: Richard C. Owen.

Graves, D. 1982. *Build a literate classroom.* Portsmouth, NH: Heinemann.

Graves, D. 1983. *Writing: Teachers and children at work.* Portsmouth, NH: Heinemann.

Harste, J.C. , V.A. Woodward, & C.L. Burke. 1984. *Language stories and literary lessons.* Portsmouth, NH: Heinemann

Holdaway, D. 1979. *Foundations of literacy.* Sydney, Australia: Ashton Scholastic.

Hubbard R. 1987. Transferring images: Not just glued on the page. *Young Children* 42 (2): 61–67

Hubbard, R. 1989. *Authors of pictures, draughtsmen of words.* Portsmouth, NH: Heinemann.

Kellogg, R. with S. O'Dell. 1967. *The psychology of children's art. Psychology Today* book. New York: CRM-Random House.

Korzenik, D. 1985. *Drawn to art.* Hanover, NH: University Press of New England.

Lasky, L., & R. Mukerji. 1980. *Art: Basic for young children.* Washington, DC: NAEYC.

Richardson, E.S. 1964. *In the early world: Discovering art through crafts.* New York: Pantheon.

Schiller, M. 1995. An emergent art curriculum that fosters understanding. *Young Children* 50 (3): 33–38.

Schirrmacher, R. 1986. Talking with young children about their art. *Young Children* 41 (5): 3–7.

Seefeldt, C. 1995. Art—A serious work. *Young Children* 50 (3): 39–45.

Wolf, A.D. 1990. Art postcards—another aspect of your aesthetics program? *Young Children* 45 (2): 39–43.

Early years are learning years

Become a member of NAEYC, and help make them count!

Just as you help young children learn and grow, the National Association for the Education of Young Children—your professional organization—supports you in the work you love. NAEYC is the world's largest early childhood education organization, with a national network of local, state, and regional Affiliates. We are more than 100,000 members working together to bring high-quality early learning opportunities to all children from birth through age eight.

Since 1926, NAEYC has provided educational services and resources for people working with children, including:

- ***Young Children***, the award-winning journal (six issues a year) for early childhood educators
- **Books, posters, brochures, and videos** to support your work with young children and families
- **The NAEYC Annual Conference**, which brings tens of thousands of people together from across the country and around the world to share their expertise and ideas on the education of young children
- **Insurance plans** for members and programs
- **A voluntary accreditation system** to help programs reach national standards for high-quality early childhood education
- **Young Children International** to promote global communication and information exchanges
- **www.naeyc.org**—a dynamic Website with up-to-date information on all of our services and resources

To join NAEYC

To find a complete list of membership benefits and options or to join NAEYC online, visit **www.naeyc.org/membership.** Or you can mail this form to us.

(Membership must be for an individual, not a center or school.)

Name ____

Address ______________________________________

City________________ State_____ ZIP___________

E-mail _______________________________________

Phone (H) _______________ (W)________________

❒ New member

❒ Renewal ID # ____________________________

Affiliate name/number ________________________

To determine your dues, you must visit **www.naeyc.org/membership** or call 800-424-2460, ext. 2002.

Indicate your payment option

❒ VISA ❒ MasterCard

Card # _______________________________________

Exp. date ____________________________________

Cardholder's name _____________________________

Signature ____________________________________

Note: By joining NAEYC you also become a member of your state and local Affiliates.

Send this form and payment to

NAEYC
PO Box 97156
Washington, DC 20090-7156